MAGNIFI~

CAT

The author wishes to thank Woman magazine for permission
to use those cartoons from this selection which originally
appeared in Woman

To Pud

Published by William Collins Sons and Co Ltd
First published 1977
Copyright © Woman magazine 1977
Printed in Great Britain

ISBN 0 00 410327 0

MAGNIFI~

A continuation of CAT-alogue
(first published 1976)

Bruce Angrave

Collins Glasgow and London

Purr-ly Queen

Not a-mew-sed

Skip-purr

Ze-fur

Down-paw

Com-fur-ter

Pro-purr-sition

Flap-purr

Purr-liceman

Puss-tor

Fur-st Noel

Last Puss-t

Paw-t

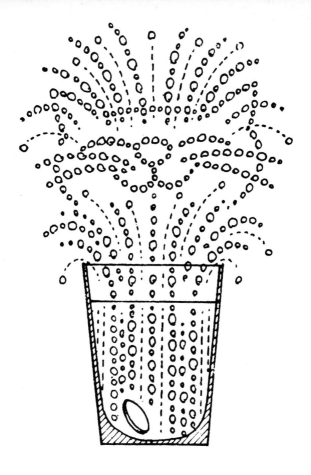

Ef-fur-vescent

Purr-oxide

Miles-purr-Hour

Royal Mews

Purr-iwig

Ap-purr-ition

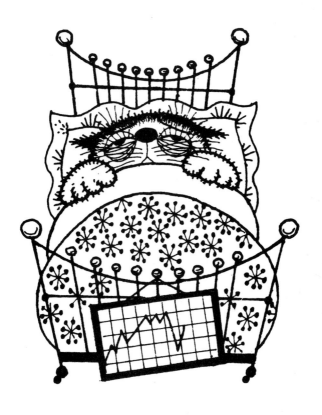

Paw-ly

T.V. Purr-sonality

Purr-dah

Can o-purr-ner

Puss-t Prandial

Pa-puss

Purr-ambulator

S-paw-ran

Purr-os-purr-ous

Chairman Miaow

Purr-goda

Big Dip-purr

Be-mew-sed

Claw-dius

Tem-puss Fugit

O-purr-a

Sleeping Tabby-lets

Purr-ch

Fur-ious

Flip-purr-s

In-fur-m

Pep-purr

S-moggy

Ves-purr-s

Hip-purr-potamus

Com-mew-ter

Im-mew-red

Dr. Henry Kit-singer

Puss-e Partout

Paw-k pie

Paw-nch

Cam-puss

Mew-tineer

Lamp-puss-t

Puss-h bike

Purr-suer

Purr-ennial

S-paw-tsman

Puss-ture

O-puss

Full Mew-n

Four Puss-ter